A NOTE TO PARENTS ABOUT DISOBEYING

"Because I told you so!" is, in most cases, an insufficient motivation for children to obey their parents. Like adults, children want and need to know the rationale behind requests they are expected to fulfill.

The purpose of this book is to help children understand the basis for parental authority. In addition, it explains the importance of being obedient and tells children how to rectify situations in which they have disobeyed.

Reading and discussing this book with your child will motivate him or her to choose obedience over disobedience. It should also decrease your need to be a disciplinarian and will give you more time to be the loving, supportive parent you want to be.

Most disobedience can be avoided by making sure children know exactly what is expected of them. Disobedience can also be avoided by involving children in the formulation of the rules and regulations for which they are responsible. Children, like adults, are more willing to comply with self-imposed guidelines rather than ones that are externally imposed. Therefore, any time invested in making your child's good behavior a team effort will result in less time spent on discipline and punishment.

A Children's Book About

DISOBEYING

Managing Editor: Ellen Klarberg
Copy Editor: Annette Gooch
Editorial Assistant: Lana Eberhard
Art Director: Jennifer Wiezel
Production Artist: Gail Miller
Illustration Designer: Bartholomew
Inking Artist: Berenice Happé Iriks
Coloring Artist: Berenice Happé Iriks
Lettering Artist: Linda Hanney
Typographer: Communication Graphics

Printed in the U.S.A.

A Children's Book About

DISOBEYING

By Joy Berry

GROLIER ENTERPRISES CORP.

This book is about Annie.

Reading about Annie can help you understand and deal with ***disobeying.***

I ASKED YOU NOT TO GET INTO THE COOKIES. I HOPE YOU ARE NOT DISOBEYING ME.
Cookie

You are disobeying when you do not do what you have been told to do.

Your parents have good reasons for telling you what to do. This is why you should not disobey them.

IF YOU EAT A COOKIE **NOW**, YOU WON'T WANT TO EAT YOUR DINNER.
SIGH!
HOW ABOUT JUST A NIBBLE?

Your parents tell you what to do because they do not want you to hurt yourself or others.

ANNIE! WAIT!
I TOLD YOU NOT TO GO INTO THE STREET!
SCREECH!

Your parents tell you what to do because they do not want you to damage or destroy things.

AUGHHH
I TOLD YOU **NOT** TO PLAY SO ROUGHLY WITH YOUR THINGS.
I HOPE SHE **DOESN'T** WANT TO PLAY WITH **ME**!
GULP!

Your parents tell you what to do because
they want you to be liked by other people.

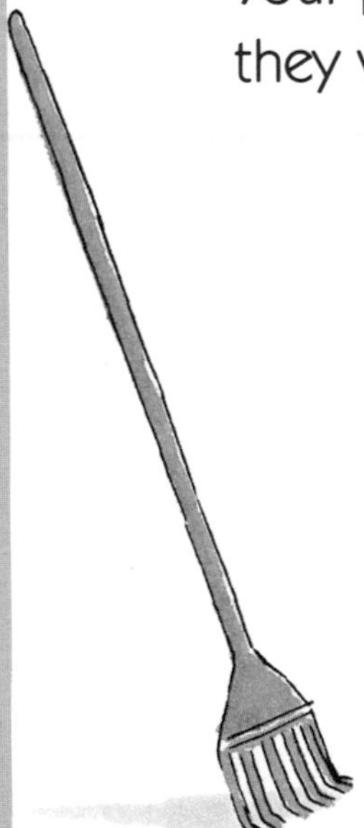

THEY WON'T PLAY WITH ME!
I TOLD YOU THAT YOU HAVE TO BE KIND TO THE OTHER CHILDREN IF YOU WANT THEM TO PLAY WITH YOU.
HMMM... SO THAT'S HOW IT WORKS.

Your parents tell you what to do because they want you to be fair.

I ASKED YOU TO PICK UP YOUR TOYS. IT ISN'T FAIR FOR YOU TO PLAY WITH THE TOYS AND THEN LEAVE THEM FOR SOMEONE ELSE TO PICK UP.
GULP

Sometimes you might wonder why parents get to tell their children what to do.

WHY DO MOM AND DAD GET TO BOSS ME AROUND? WHY CAN'T I BE MY OWN BOSS?
YEAH, **WHY**? JUST BECAUSE THEY'RE BIGGER?
TOYS

Parents tell their children what to do because they have lived longer and have learned more than children.

Thus, parents usually know what is best for their children.

OH NO, ANNIE!
I TOLD YOU NOT TO TOUCH THE HOT STOVE.
EE-OUCH!

Parents tell their children what to do because they are responsible for their children.

Parents have to take care of the damage when their children hurt themselves or others.

HOW MUCH DO I OWE THE DOCTOR FOR TAKING CARE OF ANNIE'S BURN?

Sometimes parents need to punish their children for disobeying.

The purpose of a punishment is to make children feel bad about disobeying so they will not disobey again.

I WISH DAD HADN'T TAKEN MY BIKE AWAY JUST BECAUSE I WAS RIDING IT IN THE STREET! WHEN I GET IT BACK, I WON'T RIDE IT IN THE STREET BECAUSE I DON'T WANT TO HAVE IT TAKEN AWAY AGAIN.

You can avoid being punished if you do these things:

- Talk to your parents.
- Find out what they want you to do. Then do it.

ANNIE, I DON'T WANT YOU TO EAT CANDY BEFORE DINNER.
UH-OH!
DRAT!
CHOCO-BITS

Sometimes you might not agree with your parents. Tell them how you feel.

They might change their minds. If they do not change their minds, drop the subject.

Nagging and throwing tantrums will only frustrate you and make your parents angry.

CAN'T I EAT SOME CANDY BEFORE DINNER, IF I EAT ONLY A LITTLE BIT?
NO! EVEN A LITTLE BIT OF CANDY WILL TAKE AWAY YOUR APPETITE FOR DINNER.
MAYBE I SHOULD HOLD IT UNTIL AFTER DINNER.

Tell the truth if you disobey.

Admit that you disobeyed.

Say that you are sorry and mean it.

DID YOU EAT THIS CANDY?
YES.
YOU SHOULD HAVE LET ME HOLD IT.

Accept your punishment if you disobey.

Do not be angry at your parents when they punish you. Remember, it was you who disobeyed, not them.

Try not to disobey again.

SINCE YOU DISOBEYED, YOU WILL NOT BE ALLOWED TO EAT THE REST OF THE CANDY.
SIGH!
OH, NO.

When you obey, you please your parents, and you are doing what is best for you.

HUG!
GOOD-BYE!